# The Swim

# William D. Van Atta Jr.

# Dedication

To my mom, dad, three brothers, and three sisters for all their loving support over the years. To the many precious furry and winged companions I have had the honor of experiencing life with.

# Acknowledgment

I would like to give special thanks to my mom, who introduced me to the poems of her grandfather, Joseph Russell Taylor, and his acquaintance, Robert W. Service.

Thank you to the many teachers who patiently helped me with my deficient reading and writing skills.

For introducing me to the north woods, I would like to thank the Whiteways—Dr. Robert (Red) and his wife, Marion. I worked my way through college as the Whiteways' handyman.

# About the Author

William (Bill) D. Van Atta Jr. is a veteran Army aviator and retired registered nurse who is a native of the Midwest, now living in La Crescent, Minnesota. Bill holds a Bachelor of Science degree in Geography from the University of Wisconsin–La Crosse.

After 12 years of service in the U.S. Army as both a rotary-wing and fixed-wing aviator, Bill went back to school. He graduated from The Norfolk General Hospital School of Nursing and then completed his Bachelor of Science in nursing degree at Excelsior University. He was licensed as an RN and worked in Level 1 and 2 trauma centers, where he specialized in the care of surgical, trauma, and burn patients.

When not writing, Bill enjoys spending time with his dogs. He especially likes being outdoors camping, hiking, and photographing nature. Over the past couple of years, Bill has been putting his woodworking skills to the test by building a small sailboat. He is an avid swimmer and has competed in several open water swimming competitions.

You can connect with Bill at: running_wolf57@yahoo.com.

The crowd chanted, "5, 4, 3, 2, 1!" The air horn blasted, and I advanced in a wave of swimmers across the beach and into the frigid, clear waters of Lake Superior. The shock of the icy water felt like pins and needles on the bare skin not protected by the wetsuit.

As a kid, I remember playing with my brothers and sisters in the waters at Washburn City Campground, just south of Bayfield Wisconsin. We would jump off the end of the dock and race back. Your body would be numb by the time you reached shore. We would shiver, laugh, run to the dock's end, and do it again.

I took a few strokes, then slowly settled into a rhythm. Feeling a bit anxious, I collided with several swimmers on my way to the float marking the first turn. My brain generated thoughts: Why are you doing this? Just turn around and get out.

I kept going, rounded the first marker, and entered the open water. This was my fourth year taking part in the Bayfield, Point to La Pointe event. It began in Bayfield and finished at Madeline, one of the Apostle Islands a distance of 2.1 miles.

This year, my sister Sylvia and Brothers Tim and Tom joined me, along with about 600 others. As I stroked along, thoughts about my life took me back to where my love affair with water began.

My first memory of swimming was when I was four years old, taking lessons. My dad was an elementary school physical education teacher, and one of his many specialties was aquatics. He taught me how to swim, giving me this wonderful lifetime gift.

My skills developed quickly, and by age seven, I was competing as a member of the team my dad started—University Swim Club. We worked out year-round in the 20-yard pool at the Old Armory on the campus of the University of Iowa. We always parked in the gravel lot behind The Old Armory, then walked around the building and entered the pool through a side door. You had to ascend a few steps to get to the pool.

On the wall to the left of the doorway hung a gas mask next to some large yellow cylinders labeled CHLORINE GAS. Further to the left was the room that housed the water filter system for the pool. I am not sure who handled pool maintenance, but the water was always warm and clear. However, it was probably over-chlorinated. The exposure bleached our Speedos yes, I am a recovering Speedo wearer. It also lightened and shined our hair, and because we did not wear goggles, our eyes would burn.

Not only did our eyes burn, but our sight became foggy, and psychedelic yellow-green halos appeared around bright objects. Although the water was clear and clean, this was not the case for the pool bottom. There was a collection of debris scattered in the depths. It was a conglomeration of dirt, clumps of hair, an occasional Band-Aid, and rare treasures of coins and jewelry.

Before my dad let us kids into the pool, he would go inside and make a quick check for the presence of others. Occasionally, he would forget to check, and we would be exposed to a naked Dr. Oppenheimer. He was a professor who usually swam before our practice began. He swam by himself in the buff. It was more than once that we saw his skinny, naked body rinsing off in the poolside showers. This time, my dad checked, and all was clear.

There were a couple of locker rooms and a small office in the facility. On a bulletin board by the office window that opened to the pool was a poem on a well-worn sheet of yellowing paper. We often would read it and laugh. It still holds true and makes me chuckle when I read it.

# The Swimming Pool
## Tony Lerma

The swimming pool is deep and cold.
The gutters are filled with spit and mold.
The smell on the benches is really neat,
It smells like the scum on a dead man's feet.

The chlorine in the pool is really swell.
If it gets in your eyes, it burns like hell.
It makes no difference if you're fat or thin
If you swim in chlorine, it'll rot your skin.

"First group up!" is the famous cry.
It makes you wanna stop and die.
Fifty-eight hundreds will be our fate,
So we might be out by half past eight.

"Five more to go," and the feeling's fine,
But look at the clock it's half past nine.
Practice is over "Yeah baby, cool,"
At least we're free from the swimming pool.

# The Swimming Pool

The swimming pool is deep and cold.
The gutters are filled with spit and mold.
The smell on the benches is really neat,
It smells like the scum on a dead man's feet.
The chlorine in the pool is really swell,
If it gets in your eyes it burns like hell,
It makes no difference if you're fat or thin.
If you swim in chlorine it'll rot your skin.
"First group up!" is the famous cry,
It makes you wana stop and die,
Fifty-eight hundreds will be our fate,
So we might be out by half past

I was about a half mile out and still a little bit anxious, almost panicky. I stopped, did a few breaststrokes, and then sensed a swimmer to my left. I raised my head and looked in that direction. I recognized the stroke. It was Sylvia! She put her head up and asked how I was doing. I told her, not too well, but that I should be able to make it. I had been plagued with anxiety since my time in the Army, and recently it was surfacing during open water swims. Most of the time, I was able to work through it. She gave me some encouragement, then swam on ahead. I took a few more resting strokes, adjusted my "TheMagic5" custom-fitted goggles, and then continued toward the island.

I remember the day Dad introduced us to goggles. They were blue, crude, and bulky. It took a lot of adjusting to get a good fit. They were very prone to leaking and left marks on your face from the tight strap. Out of the water, the field of view was restricted; submerged, it was even worse. The light refracted differently underwater, making your vision double, like looking cross-eyed. This took some getting used to. They did offer protection from the harsh chlorine. We only used them for workouts. They were not good enough to wear in competition. It would be a couple more years until we had goggles well enough for meets.

I celebrated my seventh birthday and soon after swam in my first meet. It took place in Moline, Illinois. I competed in several events in the 8-and-under age group. I placed sixth in one event and received my first award a pink ribbon. I was not happy about my performance or the pink ribbon and was determined to do better next time.

As best I recall, we competed in meets every couple of weeks that summer. By season's end, I had accumulated a few trophies, medals, and several ribbons. I neatly displayed them with that first pink ribbon on a shelf above the radiator in my room.

I recall one meet at the Iowa City Recreation Center when a fellow competitor got sick on me as we were being marshaled into heats. I was rushed to the shower where I rinsed off, then ran to make it just in time for my swim.

A couple of years went by. I was becoming a well-rounded swimmer. I excelled most in the longer-distance freestyle events. During this period, my dad completed his dissertation and was awarded a PhD. From that point on, he was Dr. Van Atta, but everyone soon referred to him as "Doc."

Fourth grade was my last year attending University Elementary School in Iowa City. My dad accepted a position as a professor in Physical Education at the University of Wisconsin–La Crosse (UW-L). We spent a lot of the summer shuttling household items to La Crosse. I made several trips in the old green bus my dad was converting to a camper.

My family was large seven kids, four boys and three girls so we had a lot to move. It was a four-hour journey to La Crosse, and without a new home, we put everything we could into storage. The storage building was a former funeral home. It was dark and creepy. There were items like embalming equipment and an old casket lid that had been left behind.

Across the street was Henry's, 15-Cent Hamburgers. I spent a lot of spare change there over the years.

I was starting to feel more comfortable and picked up the pace. I lifted my head every few strokes to make sure I was on course. If you strayed, you were met by a safety kayaker and redirected. I passed the orange halfway marker and could easily see where the finish line was. It was marked by a large smoke fire that was clearly visible.

Summer was over. We settled into our new home in La Crosse and started at a new school Campus School at the University of Wisconsin–La Crosse. It was my first day as a fifth grader. My dad escorted me to the classroom, where I was welcomed by Mrs. Johnson and several students. I was shown my desk, and the school year was off to a start.

There was no formal swimming team for kids in La Crosse, but I soon learned about a small group of boys who worked out at the YMCA. The building was built in 1909, and it had a 15-yard pool in the basement. It was crowded and chaotic trying to swim in the small pool.

My dad soon became involved, and with his expertise, things became more organized. The girls had a similar situation they swam in the indoor pool at the Bluff View Motel. To supplement our training, we would swim at the university with my dad in one of Wittich Hall's 20-yard pools.

A new YM/YWCA was soon under construction. It included a beautiful 25-yard, 6-lane pool. The new pool soon became home to the La Crosse Y Swim Team. My dad was head coach. He was helped by several assistant coaches and dedicated parents.

In the summer, we would use the city's Erickson and Memorial pools. These pools were not heated, and they remained icy cold through most of the summer. We swam in the early morning, and by the time the workout was over, your teeth chattered and your frozen body shook uncontrollably.

I swam on. The water was calm and flat, with just a light breeze. There was an occasional wave, probably coming from the Madeline Island Ferry operating just south of the course. I was hit by a wave as I was taking a breath and took in a mouthful of water. I had to stop to clear my airway and catch my breath. I started back up and headed for the finish line. I thought, no guts, no glory.

The sign on the locker room wall in Wittich Hall read in bold black letters, "No Guts, No Glory." I glanced up at it, then headed upstairs to the pool. I was training for the Quincy YMCA Swim Marathon with my dad and sisters, Molly and Sylvia. The swim covered a 10-mile stretch of the Mississippi from La Grange, Missouri, to Quincy, Illinois. We trained every day, sometimes twice. I would occasionally get painful cramps in my legs and would be forced to take a break.

It was time. We rode the old green bus to Quincy and spent the night crowded into a Holiday Inn. For our race day breakfast, my dad insisted that we have steak and eggs. We were shuttled to the start area, where we put on our suits and lathered on some baking grease for insulation. Then, sequenced one after another, we entered the muddy Mississippi and began our swim downstream.

Each swimmer had a safety boat with a driver and a lookout. My lookout was one of my school friends. The river was near flood stage with a strong current, so the race times were fast. I think most completed the swim in less than two hours. That was the second time I did the swim and the last. The event was not held after that.

I did swim in the Black River swim that was held one year. It was five miles, running from the Airport Beach on French Island to the Big Indian at Riverside Park in La Crosse. I did not swim in any more marathons after that but continued to concentrate on the distance events. I stayed on the Y team through high school. There was no high school swim team or a pool. I did run some cross country and track, but by my junior year, I gave it up for swimming.

A pair of inverted kicking feet suddenly appeared in front of me. Fortunately, I stopped quickly enough to avoid a kick to the face. As I stopped and raised my head, cramps attacked my legs. I found myself facing a young woman doing elementary backstroke. She was in a little distress and said she was seasick. I told her I had leg cramps, then moved on. I was able to change my stroke to lessen the pain. The cramps subsided, and I picked up the pace. I was feeling tired but good. I could clearly see the smoke and people near the finish. The adrenaline was kicking in.

My signature event: the 1650 nearly a mile in a 25-yard pool. I was a college sophomore at UW–L, swimming in the Wisconsin State University Conference Championships. I was about 1,000 yards into the race and not far from the lead swimmers. I hit my turn perfectly, came off the wall, and was consumed by a surge of energy. It was like a switch was flipped. I scanned my competitors and, to my surprise, saw that I was in front. I felt no pain and stroked away effortlessly. I could see my teammates running along the poolside, cheering me on. The lap gun fired two lengths to go. I felt goosebumps all the way to the finish. I touched the wall. I was conference champion.

That was my best performance ever. The summer after my victory, I trained at the University of Iowa's Intensive Swim Camp. Swimmers of all ages trained there, including an Australian Olympian. We swam three workouts a day, averaging 15 to 18 thousand yards daily. Eat, sleep, swim, and repeat. I was in the best condition of my life, but my junior and senior years were plagued by illness, burnout, and great disappointment.

I graduated from college, went into the Army, and took up running. When I was deployed to Saudi Arabia in support of Desert Shield and then Desert Storm, I decided to try a little swimming to supplement my running. I swam in the small pool at the compound where I stayed.

Soon I was relocated to King Khalid Military City (KKMC), in the middle of the desert. The city was very ornate, with gardens and fountains. It reminded me of the Emerald City from *The Wizard of Oz*. I was able to find an unused 50-meter indoor pool in the heart of the city. I swam there a few times before the war started and shut the facility down.

One afternoon, I entered the pool, and behind me, two heavily armed soldiers appeared. They checked the area, then a man emerged in a swimsuit. I recognized him as one of the generals we regularly flew, Lieutenant General Pagonis. I completed my swim in the presence of the general and his bodyguards, then returned to my quarters to await the next mission.

I left the Army and started swimming regularly again when a fitness center opened in the community where I lived. I have continued to swim since then, taking the gift with me wherever I go.

Just a few hundred yards to go I could smell the smoke from the signal fire. I could hear music and the PA announcing the finishing participants. The sandy bottom came into view. I rounded the final marker and fell in line behind some other finishers. I climbed up the exit stairs and staggered across the finish line. I smiled and sighed in relief.

I changed out of my wetsuit, then joined family and friends. We reminisced about our past swimming experiences and gave credit to all who had helped us along the way. Then we made our way to the ferry that would take us back to where the adventure began.

I stood at the shore, looked back at Madeline Island, and with a grin thought that, just like the swim, life wasn't about winning a pink ribbon, a medal, not even a trophy but about the journey and sharing it with family and friends.

*"Keep Swimming! "*

www.ingramcontent.com/pod-product-compliance
Lightning Source LLC
Chambersburg PA
CBHW041130120626
46547CB00019B/2927